TO HELL *WITH* TITLES *GIVE* THEM LEADERSHIP

A PARABLE ABOUT **UNLEASHING** YOUR LEADERSHIP **GREATNESS**

Khalid Asad, Leadership Storyteller

Published by Performance Plus International, Inc.

1800 Diagonal Road, Suite 600 Diagonal Road, Alexandria, VA

www.ppiinc.net

Cover by Troy Lambert.

ISBN 978-1-66782-846-6 eBook 978-1-66782-847-3

Printed in the United States of America

CONTENTS

DEDICATION

To my grandmother, Rose Phillips, thank you for teaching me the importance of having faith, vision, and, most importantly, the ability to love.

To my mother, Joyce Phillips-Frazier, you taught me the importance of building meaningful relationships. You instilled in me the determination to keep going no matter the obstacle, to get up after every fall.

To my sister, Ravella McGann, from you, I learned not to be limited by our disabilities but rather to focus on our abilities and the contributions we want to make to our communities and the world in general.

Thank you all. May you continue to rest in peace.

Preface

Think about the manager you work with or those you've previously worked for. For some, you may think, *"This person is a great leader."* Others may cause you to raise one eyebrow and ask, *"Whose idea was it to give this person the keys to the leadership mobile?"* I am sure that you can differentiate between the two. One energizes you, which in turn allows for inspiring and meaningful contributions, while the other causes you to break the sick leave or vacation bank while you search for your next opportunity. While the former approach their leadership role with humility and grace, the latter wield their title like a sharp sword that pierces the heart of the committed and shreds the desires and hopes of those wanting worthwhile participation.

In my thirty years of serving in leadership roles or training and coaching others on improving their leadership effectiveness, I have seen first-hand the effects of both leadership styles mentioned above. This book is based on my experiences and scholarly research about effective leadership. I share with you Five Cs essential to leadership while painting a practical picture that allows you to relate to the concepts and apply them to your situation or context.

This book is written for anyone who has questions about what it means to lead. It speaks to all who may be hesitant, thinking they may not possess inherent leadership qualities or feel they do not have the prestige or credentials to influence others or drive change. It will not only make you examine the leadership of others, but it will compel you to look critically at yourself and decide the type of leader you want to be and the kind of experience you want others to have when interacting with you. It dispels the long-standing myth that title or status makes someone an effective leader. You will feel confident in acting out of a sense of purpose and vision and inspiring others to do the same to be a part of something special and impactful.

I have written Jim Reynolds' story as a parable, allowing you to relate to the story personally. It should encourage you to reflect on your leadership journey and consider the effect you would like to have on the people you serve, your workplace, and the larger community. It breathes life into the 'leadership conversation' and allows you to imagine what leadership could be like if you discover and embrace the leader within you. As you read Jim's story, think about people you know who were asked to lead but were hesitant or felt unready yet bravely stepped up in ways that had a tremendous impact on those around them and the mission of their organizations.

Please take note and consider how Jim embraced the Five C's, based on advice from an unlikely coach, to strengthen his ability to influence others and transform his team and organization. You can apply these principles despite your title or status when leading others. My wish is that Jim's story becomes your story.

Chapter One: Uncertainty and Opportunity at DCFS

It's late on a Friday evening; Jim Reynolds is in his office, gathering his belongings, when his phone rings.

"Division of Children and Family Services Operations, Jim Reynolds speaking, how may I help you?"

"Jim, this is Rebecca. Can I see you in my office?"

Rebecca White is the Division of Children and Family Services (DCFS) Executive Director. She was brought in six months ago to clean up the agency.

Never having spoken to Rebecca, he nervously replies,

"Certainly, I'll be right there."

Making his way to her office, his mind wonders, *"Why does she want to meet with me?"*

Since Rebecca began her tenure, she has restructured the agency, fired individuals, and demoted others. Arriving at Rebecca's office, he knocks.

"Come in, Jim."

He enters, and she invites him to join her at the conference table.

"Jim, as you may have heard, I'm very direct.

Jim smiles but says nothing.

So, I will get straight to the point. I would like you to take over the Operations Division."

"What happened to Rob?" he asks with a puzzled look.

Rob, Jim's boss, has been with the agency for twenty-seven years.

"I asked him to step down; he is considering his options. I have heard good things about your commitment and dedication; you are knowledgeable and understand how the other divisions work. I need you to take the reins of the Operations Division and turn things around."

Jim knows that Operations is the engine that allows DCFS to run smoothly. It includes Information Technology, Human Resources, Staff Development, Transportation, as well as other services.

"This is a huge responsibility, Rebecca, and we haven't always received the support we require. I need time to consider what you're asking me to do."

"Okay, let me know by Monday. I know it is not much time, but I need to let the mayor know that my leadership team is in place and that progress is being made. I am counting on you to step up."

"Oh great, this is political!" He stands, thanks Rebecca for the opportunity, and heads for the door. It is going to be a long weekend! He boards the 7:15 pm train, his mind filled with questions. *"Why was Rob demoted? Why did Rebecca choose me? What happens if I refuse? What can I do to turn things around in the division?"*

"K street station coming up!" the train's loudspeaker announces. *"That was fast."* His thoughts so consumed him that the ride home seemed much shorter than usual.

Arriving home, Jim finds his wife, Pam, and their two children, Marcia and Ben, watching TV in the family room. Marcia, eleven, and Ben, aged nine, happy to see their dad, hug him. A tired but happy Jim, buoyed by his children's affections, kisses his wife. Jim enjoys spending time with his wife and children and tries to ensure nothing interferes with 'family time.' After dinner, he kisses his children 'goodnight' and joins Pam in their bedroom. While preparing for bed, Jim and his wife discuss his encounter with Rebecca; Pam assures him that he has her full support with whichever decision he makes.

After a long weekend filled with family fun and decision-making struggles, Jim arrives at work early on Monday morning. He logs onto his computer, grabs a cup of coffee, and heads to Rebecca's office. When he arrives, he's not surprised to find her already working. He knocks on the open door,

"Good morning, Rebecca."

"Good morning, Jim; how was your weekend?"

"Aside from struggling with my decision about your request, it was great."

"Well?"

"I gave it much thought and decided to accept your offer. However, I have two questions. First, when do you want me to start?"

"I need you to begin immediately. I cannot afford to have Operations run another day without someone at the helm. There are key initiatives that require the division's support."

"May I have a week to transition?"

"Certainly, Jim, that is not a problem."

"Great! My next question is exactly what you mean by 'turn things around?'"

"Jim, we all know that the Operations Division has been underperforming for some time. I need you to hold people accountable. You'll figure it out, but my approach is to let people know what I expect from them and that I am in charge. It has not failed me yet."

Smiling at Rebecca, he grabs his coffee and gets up to leave.

"Thank you for the opportunity. I'll keep you posted on how things are going."

"Be sure you do."

Chapter Two: Taking the Reins

Being the boss is different from being the leader!

After spending the past week transitioning into his new responsibilities, Jim prepares to meet with his team. The meeting is scheduled for 10:00 a.m. in what was Rob's conference room. Jim is a little nervous, as the staff attending were his colleagues only last week, and he is now their boss, and as Rebecca reminded him, she expects him to take charge. Jim grabs a notepad and heads to the conference room. On his way there, a couple of people congratulate him on his promotion. He responds with a smile and a thank you but thinks, *"Don't congratulate me yet; I could end up like Rob."*

Jim arrives at the conference room to find Stacey Moss, the IT manager, who is already there.

"Good morning, Jim."

"Good morning, Stacey. How are you?"

"I'm fine. I want to get this meeting over with; I have more important things on my plate.

Jim smiles but does not respond to her comment. Stacey is well known for being a bit brash, confrontational, and very protective of her people and turf. She has no filter; if she thinks it, she says it. Looking at the clock, she announces,

It's five minutes after ten, and they are all late as usual. If you can fix that issue, I will name you the manager of the year," she says sarcastically.

At a loss for words, Jim replies,

"Let's give them a few more minutes."

No sooner than the words have left his mouth, Juan, Ali, and Priscilla enter the room, sounding like a chorus, "Sorry, sorry we're late."

"Jim, you know this is part of our team's culture; no one gets to a meeting on time; 10:00 means 10:15," Juan adds.

Jim does not respond. After everyone settles, he kicks off the meeting.

"As you may know, Rebecca has asked me to step into Rob's role. Am I thrilled? I am unsure, but Rebecca wanted someone to turn things around."

"And she asked you?" Juan enquires jokingly.

"Seriously, if I don't turn things around, I could be out on my butt just like Rob."

"What does she mean by 'turn things around?" Ali, who oversees Staff Development, asks.

"I am not sure, but I need a list of all key initiatives you're working on." "When would you like our lists?" asks Stacey.

"I need them by Friday."

"That's too soon, screams Priscilla, the Director of Human Resources.

I need to prepare for Thursday's Labor-Management meeting."

"I know my request is short notice, but the information is needed by

Friday, I want to understand how we benefit the agency and what we can do differently."

"We don't need to do anything differently; we are doing great," suggests Juan.

Jim looks at each person in turn; his gaze falls on Juan.

"Are you sure about that, Juan? So why was Rob demoted? Jim pauses to allow them time to ponder his question.

Are there any other questions or comments?

He is greeted with silence as everyone gazes at their notepads.

Okay, let's meet here at 10:00 a.m. on Friday."

Back in his office, Jim reflects upon the meeting and wonders how the others view him. *"Will they work for me? How did the division get such a bad reputation? Why didn't Rob hold people accountable? What can I do to make them take me seriously?"* He is interrupted by the telephone.

"DCFS, Operations Division, Jim Reynolds speaking."

"Jim, this is Rebecca. Did you have an opportunity to meet with your team?"

"Yes, I met with them this morning."

"How did it go?"

"Things went well."

"Good, I want you to know I am counting on you to turn things around. I don't want to make any more management changes," she emphasizes.

"I understand."

"Well, I'll let you get back to work. Keep me posted on how things progress."

"I will. Take care, Rebecca."

Jim spends the rest of his day reading Rob's old files, checking emails, and scheduling meetings. The remainder of the week takes on a similar tone and routine. He also meets with other members of the Operations staff.

It is 09:55 on Friday morning. Jim is sitting in the conference room awaiting his team. At 10:00 as he gets up from his seat to check on their whereabouts Juan and Ali walk in together. They both confess they forgot about the meeting.

Jim does not respond. Using the conference room phone, he calls Priscilla and Stacey. By 10:30 a.m., everyone is present.

"We've got to do something about starting our meetings on time, says a frustrated Jim. I know this is how we operated when Rob was here, but this is unacceptable. I wasted thirty minutes waiting for you." No one says a word. Stacey churlishly chimes in,

"It was your idea to hold a meeting on a Friday. No one meets on Fridays, and besides, I did not have time to pull together a list of IT projects."

"I didn't pull mine together either," Juan adds.

Jim turns his gaze to the other members of his team,

"How about you, Ali? Priscilla?

They both shake their heads. Jim, furious and frustrated, goes on a tirade. His colleagues have never seen this side of him.

Let's get something straight; when I ask you all to do something, I expect you to do it. I am in charge of this division, which means I am your boss. So, here's what is going to happen. I'm going to reschedule this meeting for Monday at 9:00 a.m. Everyone better get here on time with your list in hand. If you are late or do not have your list, don't bother showing up. I'll deal with you later.

You got me?

He slams his folder on the table. Everyone nods in unison.

Do you have any questions for me?"

The silence is deafening.

A demoralized Jim walks out of the conference room, heads straight to his office, and calls Rebecca. Her secretary puts the call through.

"What's going on, Jim?" she asks.

"I need to take the rest of the day off."

"Is everything okay?"

"Everything is fine. I want to start fresh on Monday."

"Okay, but I'm here if you need to talk."

He declines her offer, and after checking his email, he grabs his backpack and heads for the elevator. On the way down, he thinks, *"What the hell did I get myself into?"*

As the doors open, he hears someone talking about a problem with the trains.

"Great! What else can go wrong?" he grumbles.

Jim runs toward a taxi sitting at the traffic lights. The driver sees him and waits. Jim hops into the cab and immediately shouts out his address.

"510 East Twenty-Eighth."

"I know exactly where that is, the driver responds with a thick Jamaican accent. The expressway is jammed right now, so we will have to drive through town."

"Are you serious?" asks an exasperated Jim.

"They've shut down parts of it to allow emergency vehicles to respond to the train derailment, explains the driver. We'll be in traffic for a while, but you are in good hands. I know every back road and shortcut that exists in the city."

"And I thought my terrible week was over," mutters a frustrated Jim.

"It sounds like you had a rough week."

"Huh?"

"It sounds like you had a rough week," repeats the driver.

"That would be the ultimate understatement."

"It couldn't have been that bad."

"Sir, no disrespect, but could we have a quiet ride, please? I prefer not to discuss my week."

"You don't have to call me sir; my name is Prof-I, and I've been driving cabs and observing people for some time. I can tell when someone has a lot on their plate."

"What are you talking about?"

"Jim, many people from all walks of life have sat in the back of my cab. College kids, hardworking people, CEOs, politicians, you name it. The young man who left the White House a few years back spent countless hours discussing politics, social issues, planning his team, and more. This is where he developed his vision for hope and change. You peg me as just a cab driver when you look at me. Well, Jim, you are entitled to your perceptions; they are yours."

"How do you know my name?"

"Well, either that's your badge, or you lifted it from someone else. Should I call the police, Prof-I asks with a chuckle?"

Jim smiles.

"No need for that; my week has been rough already."

"You smiled; that's healthy for the spirit. I tell you what. I want to help you."

"Help me, how can you help me?" asks Jim dubiously.

"I'm going to help in two ways," replies Prof-I. "First, I'm going to help you build trust."

"Trust?"

"Yes, I'm going to help you to trust me. Unless you trust me, I cannot help you in a second way: to help you deal with whatever's going on at work."

"How can you help me at work?"

"First, you must tell me what's happening, but not today. Please go home, relax, and let today take its rightful place in the past. Tomorrow is a new day. For me to help you, you must agree to ride my cab until you feel you have things in hand."

"I take the metro; it's cheaper."

"Cheaper than free?"

"Free?" Jim asks with incredulity.

"Yes, free! I won't charge you a dime, responds Prof-I. The only things I ask you to do is to trust, listen, be vulnerable, and be transparent.

After a brief pause and thinking that he must be crazy, Jim agrees. Realizing that he's already home; Jim reaches for his wallet but is halted by Prof-I.

Remember, we agreed that your rides are free."

Jim exits the cab, walks to the front passenger door, reaches through the window, and shakes Prof-I's hand.

"Prof-I, I don't know who you are, but I'm going to take you up on your offer. You drive safely, and I will see you Monday morning here at 7 a.m."

Prof-I smiles, nods, and drives off.

Jim walks toward his front door. Before he reaches it, the door opens, and is greeted by his wife.

"You're home early."

"I took a cab."

"You hate taking cabs," Pam says, surprised.

"The metro was shut down; the rest is a long story. Suffice it to say; that I'll be taking a cab to and from work for a while.

Pam gives him a puzzled look.

Don't ask; just trust me. Let's have lunch and relax. How are the kids?"

"They're fine; they've eaten and are in their rooms, playing and doing whatever kids do when they're on their own."

Jim spends time in each of the children's rooms before re-joining Pam in the den.

"Now tell me about your day, says Pam.

Jim shares the terse exchange he had with his team.

Oh, Jim, that doesn't sound like you!" she exclaims.

"Believe me, it felt like an out-of-body experience. It's the pressure of being told I must turn things around. I need them to take me seriously. I'm no longer their colleague; I'm their boss."

"What does that mean?"

"It means that I'm responsible for ensuring the work gets done, and they are accountable to me," he explains.

Jim takes advantage of his early arrival by spending more time with his family. Before falling asleep, Jim ruminates on his conversation with Prof-I. After an hour of restless tossing, he falls asleep.

Monday morning arrives, and Jim is standing in his living room waiting for Prof-I. He hears a car pull up. *"Wow, he's five minutes early."* He lets Pam know that he's leaving.

"Okay, honey, have a good day."

Jim gets into the cab, and Prof-I hands him a cup of coffee.

"Just the way you like it, extra cream and extra sugar."

"How did you know how I drink my coffee?"

"Attention to details, the coffee cup you had when I picked you up last week was marked EC/ES."

"Wow! I'm impressed," says Jim.

During the ride, Jim explains his new role to Prof-I and the challenges he's faced thus far: supervising people who once were his colleagues, working with a boss who's driven by results, and just trying to get things done.

"Oh boy, you do have your hands full, young man! What is it that you think people don't get?"

"My staff needs to understand that I'm the boss now," Jim says after pausing to consider his response.

"Gwaan boss mon, you run tings!" Prof-I laughingly replies.

"What does that mean?" Jim looks at him, puzzled.

Prof-I laughs again before replying.

"Inside Jamaican joke. This is a good start to our journey. We just identified your first problem. You want people to acknowledge your new status as the boss."

"Well, I am, he says petulantly; Rebecca appointed me Director of Operations."

"So, you plan to get things done through your status and title?

Jim is silent and looks puzzled.

To hell with your title, lead them. What does that mean, you ask?"

"It sounds like a corny catchphrase," replies Jim.

"Call it what you want; it will save your butt, inspire your people, and help them to help you get things done. Too often, managers want to tell people what to do. They use their status or title and, in some cases, bully people to get things done. I can give you examples of when that approach has worked, but it is always at the expense of other things, like stress, burn-out, high turnover, unhealthy work culture, and much more. You mark my words; if that's going to be your approach, you will fail miserably. The good news is I will be here for you to cry on my shoulders, Prof-I says sarcastically.

A frustrated Jim rolls his eyes and gazes out the window.

Your sentiments are not unusual, Prof-I continues. Far too often, managers feel that their titles give them the license to rule over people, treating them as their subjects rather than valuable partners or stakeholders. This selfish, controlling, and sometimes passive-aggressive approach is rewarded and has become the standard for leadership. In many cases, what managers believe deep down is manifested in their behaviors. What's sad is that these behaviors are so engrained that some managers are oblivious to them. They have lost themselves and have become the epitome of the bad bosses they once complained about. Hence, at the beginning of our journey, we will search for Jim. We will help you discover who you are and what you believe. We're going to go in search of your purpose. How will your self-discovery inform your leadership style? I never promised you that this was going to be easy. I promised free cab rides to work and that in return for your trust, I will help you to discover the leader within."

Prof-I asks Jim to think about their conversation and begin searching for his leadership identity. Jim gives Prof-I a half-hearted nod, gets out of the cab, and walks toward his building.

Chapter Three: Clarify your Convictions

Your convictions are like the GPS in your car. Will they keep you on the right path if you follow them?

Jim is in his office preparing for the meeting with his team. He is trying to concentrate on the day ahead, but he is unable to do so. Prof-I's comments gnaw at him, especially the comments about finding himself and clarifying his convictions. He recalls the conversation when Rebecca appointed him head of the division. The focus was on what is important to her and her management style; they never discussed his beliefs, what is important to him, or what he stands for. *"Maybe I'm unclear because I never thought about my purpose."*

Shaking his head, Jim returns his focus to the task at hand and makes his way to the conference room. He arrives to find the team waiting for him.

"Thank you for being on time. Before we begin, I need to apologize for my outburst last week. It was inappropriate, and I had no right to speak to you the way I did. Please accept my apology, and if you need to speak to me individually, I'll make myself available."

Jim can feel the tension in the room slowly seep away.

"I knew you didn't mean it the moment it happened. Let me apologize for not taking you seriously." Juan chimes in after a few moments of silence.

The rest of the team shares the same sentiment. With fences mended, they get down to business. Each manager shares their projects, discusses project statuses, and identifies the resources and support they need. Jim takes notes, asks questions, and agrees to elevate several pressing issues to Rebecca.

"I'm meeting with her this week; I'll add these items to our agenda. Thank you all for your feedback."

The remainder of the day is routine; Jim sits through more meetings, makes phone calls, and reviews agency data. Before he realizes it, it's 5:30 p.m. *"Where did the time go?"* He packs up his things and heads for the elevator. When he arrives out front, a horn blows, and Prof-I waves him over.

"Sorry I'm a little late," Jim says as he gets into the cab.

"No problem, mon, dere is no such ting as being late. People move when it's time to move. How was your day?"

"It was a blur; I spent the entire day thinking about the questions you asked me this morning," replies Jim.

"Oh?"

"I realize I am unclear about who I am, the important things, or what I stand for. I don't even know where to begin. Everything seems important."

"Hmm, so essentially, nothing is important."

"That's not what I said!"

"I heard what you said. When people chase everything, they catch nothing because there's no focus on their thoughts or actions. You must determine your convictions. They are like the GPS in your car; they guide your actions and warn you when you make a wrong turn or stray off course. Have you ever been in a situation where someone asks you to do something you disagree with in principle?"

"Most certainly,"

"How did you feel?"

"I felt tense, and my stomach felt tight."

"A gut feeling," suggests Prof-I.

"Exactly!"

"It sounds like you can identify. That gut feeling is your GPS telling you that you are about to violate one or more of your convictions, the same thing the GPS in your car does when you miss a turn. It tries to reroute your journey. For your GPS to work, you must enter the right destination. Jim, you must program your GPS with what you believe in or stand for. The information is there; it's based on your upbringing, your professional and personal experiences, and the things you have learned. Why did you choose this type of work? What's most important to you, and where are you in your life's journey?

Jim starts to respond.

Don't answer me; you must answer yourself. When you get settled at home, reflect on your life and make notes related to your answers to these questions. It doesn't matter what others think. It's about what you believe to be true for you."

Jim nods his head in agreement as he exits the cab.

"Thank you, Prof-I."

I'll see you tomorrow; enjoy your evening," Prof-I responds.

After dinner and some quality with the family, Jim retreats to the den to contemplate his 'core convictions.' He sits in his recliner and recalls memories of his childhood. He instinctively knows that the core of his belief system began there. His grandmother raised him after his mother died of an overdose.

She became his guiding light, helping to mold him into the man he would become. He recalls being poor and how his grandmother struggled to provide even the basics; despite this, she taught him the importance of supporting others. Jim recalls conversations he had with her; even now, he could still hear his grandmother's voice.

"Grandma, one day, I'm going to be rich, and we'll be able to buy anything we want!"

"What about the people around you, Jimmy? If they're not okay, then the community is not okay."

Whenever he got into arguments with other children,

"Jimmy, be respectful."

"Well, they don't respect me," he would retort.

"Regardless of how others behave, you must always do what you know is right. That means you may endure pain, ridicule, and humiliation. Use it as a motivator. This will make you a better man. Don't compromise who you are and what you stand for."

"Wow!" Jim says aloud. He puts pen to paper and jots down words that resonate with him:

Community

Respect

Support

Service

Partnerships

These qualities form his moral compass. In his personal life, they have carried him through the good times and the bad, while in his professional life, these ideals have helped him work with others to implement impactful programs and processes. By clarifying his core convictions, he can see his purpose.

"I'm here to help others be their best selves by partnering with them and helping them overcome the barriers they encounter. That's what moves me!" Jim says emphatically.

He is looking forward to sharing his breakthrough with Prof-I in the morning.

Heartened by a sense of accomplishment, Jim puts away his notes and goes to bed.

The following day, Jim wakes up to his children arguing.

"Marcia! Ben! You're going to be late for school," his wife shouts.

"She threw my backpack," responds Ben.

"I did not," Marcia retorts.

Jim rushes through his routine. In no time, he's showered, shaved, and dressed. He enters the kitchen, where the rest of the family is having breakfast, and raises an eyebrow at Ben and Marcia. The children are immediately contrite. Jim grabs a cup of coffee and bagel just as a horn blows. It's Prof-I, right on schedule.

Smiling, Jim gets into the cab.

"Good morning,"

"You're feeling irie today," replies Prof-I.

"Irie?"

"Yeah, mon, another Jamaican word for feeling good."

"I'll take irie, says Jim. I did my homework last night."

"Did you?"

"Sure did; it was the first time in a while that I sat still long enough to think. I was able to put things in perspective and identify the things that contribute to my values. Not only was I able to identify them, but I can also explain why they are important.

Jim shares each component and explains them in the context of life experiences.

Throughout my personal and professional life, I've always felt a sense of duty to help others. It isn't about handouts; sometimes, people need a fighting chance, an opportunity, support, whatever we want to call it. We are often caught up in the 'world of me,' heads down, blinders on, and entirely focused on our agendas. What about the people around us? Our families, co-workers, friends, or our community. Do we stop and think about what may be going on with the person next to us or what they need? I believe we should wake up every day and ask ourselves, 'how can we help others improve their lives?' Not judge them as 'lesser than' but see them as people who deserve to fulfill their hopes and dreams. That is why I'm here! How can I support my family and others so they can achieve their goals and dreams? This is the question I want to answer every day."

The two men are silent for a few moments, then Jim explains why his convictions are important to him. He recalls his childhood for Prof-I and wonders how different things would have been if they had the support they needed. What would have happened if his father had taken an active role in helping his grandmother raise him or, at the very least, had contributed financially? How much more effective would Rob, his former boss, have been if he had received more support from his staff, colleagues, and his manager?

"Those are great questions. As I shared with you yesterday, our convictions drive how we see the world, our interactions with others, and our decision-making. Jim, I want you to consider what you were asked to do. You were given the opportunity to lead a team, not just manage them or be their boss.

There's a significant difference between the two. Do you know what that means?"

"Sure, I do. I am supposed to make sure they have what they need to do their part in helping the agency fulfill its mission."

"But how do you plan to do that?

Jim is silent. They are only minutes from the office.

When you engage people today, I want you to keep your convictions in mind. How do they guide your actions, your words, and your decisions? Take notice of how people respond to you."

Jim exits the cab and heads into the building.

"Hold that elevator, please, he shouts. Thank you, can you please press eight?" he says to a man standing by the door.

Priscilla is waiting, with some personnel files, for Jim when he arrives at his office.

"We have pressing HR issues that need to be addressed this week and several promotions that require your signature, she informs him. We also have seven people on the Americans with Disabilities Act (ADA) list who must be placed before we get sued. There are positions available to accommodate them; the hiring managers need to comply."

Jim walks into his office and invites her to accompany him.

"Good morning, Priscilla. Come in. Let me make one phone call, and then we can spend the next hour reviewing these and making decisions, okay?"

She is stunned; she expected him to ask her to schedule a meeting later in the week. Priscilla felt Rob always blew her off when she needed to meet with him. She waits in Jim's conference room while he makes his phone call. Before long, he joins her.

"That was quick," she says.

"I didn't want to keep you waiting; I know you have a lot on your plate." She pauses for a moment, and although she doesn't say it, she feels supported. Suddenly, someone is giving her the time and audience to discuss issues important to her and her team. Over the next hour, they discuss a few unresolved HR issues and strategies for addressing them. She also gets the signoffs she needs to move forward with placing and supporting employees that require ADA accommodations. They also handle other personnel matters she brought to the meeting. Before she leaves, Jim thanks her for bringing the issues to his attention and making them a priority.

"Do you want me to run these by the legal department?" she asks.

"I don't think you need to; you made solid arguments for your decisions, and I trust your judgment. You've been doing this for more than ten years and have done homework on the issues we discussed; trust yourself."

She smiles. *"This is a first!"* He has never seen Priscilla smile. Before she leaves, she thanks him for his time, and Jim suggests they schedule bi-weekly meetings to discuss HR issues.

"I want to dedicate more time to your area."

She thanks him again and heads to her office.

Jim prints out reports in preparation for his meeting with Rebecca. He couldn't help thinking about his meeting with Priscilla. He has never seen her relaxed.

"She has always been so difficult to work with. Is she okay?"

As he continues to reflect, he notices an email in his inbox from her titled, "Thank you." He opens it. It reads,

> *Jim,*
>
> *Thank you for meeting with me this morning. I appreciate you taking the time to listen and being genuinely interested in what is going on in HR and what I had to say. All I ever wanted was someone to care about my work and help me think through some of our challenges. You have my full support in your new role. Let me know how I can help.*
>
> *He reflects on his interaction with Priscilla and recalls allowing her to drive the conversation, make decisions, and offer his support. He realizes that he was supportive of her both professionally and personally. It was so fundamental, and it felt good! Jim knows most managers fail to take the most basic actions when working with others.*
>
> *Priscilla,*

*Thank you for sharing your concerns and, more importantly,
your ideas for addressing complex issues. I look forward to
our next biweekly meeting.*

However, I'm here if you need to talk before then.

Thanks,

Jim

Jim heads to Rebecca's office for their meeting to discuss some

department-wide initiatives. When he arrives, her secretary Alice tells him to go in. Rebecca is wrapping up a phone call.

"Hi, Jim."

"Hello, Rebecca."

They exchange small talk before getting to the business at hand.

"Jim, what are your thoughts about the new service-delivery process?"

"What do you mean?"

"How do you think it's going?"

"I think it's going okay."

"Just okay, that's not good?"

"We still have much work to do. We have not put the resources into some of the key areas. For example, we are shifting many resources to quality assurance. While I understand monitoring is critical, I want to see us invest more resources in capacity building."

"Why is that?"

"Well, capacity building helps the agencies to build the infrastructure such as staff, processes, and the practices needed to support families. If we don't put the resources into these areas, the quality of the services will suffer."

"We don't have any resources to add to capacity building. Richard is requesting four additional staff for the quality reviews. I promised him that I would make it happen," Rebecca responds.

"I think he could get by with two for now. Let's face it; these reviews won't happen for another three months. We need to build capacity now, as evidenced by the mistakes and staff turnover they are experiencing. We can invest in it now or pay dearly later," says Jim.

"What does that mean?" asks Rebecca.

"It means that either we invest the resources to ensure quality on the front end, or we expend resources to clean up the poor practice revealed by the data on the back end. Practice drives quality: reviews tell us how we are doing after the fact. Let's flip the order in which we make our investments."

After a few more minutes of going back and forth, Rebecca agrees to give Jim five more people to help with capacity building. He thanks her and heads back to his office. He grabs his lunch from the refrigerator on the way.

"Hold all my calls," I need to catch up on emails and write a few reports," he says to Marie, his executive assistant.

"Okay," she says as he closes his door.

Despite getting what he needs from Rebecca, he is not overjoyed. Instead, he is a little frustrated that he had to convince her about the importance of capacity building. The remainder of the day goes by quickly before he realizes it's time to go.

Prof-I is parked in front of the building. *"Is this guy ever late?"*

"Good evening, O Masterful One," he says with a smile and faux reverence as he gets into the cab.

"Good evening, Luke," responds Prof-I.

"Luke?"

"Yes, Mr. Skywalker, I hope the force was with you today," Prof-I says jokingly.

"It was, indeed, Obi-Wan. I have much to share."

"Do share, young Skywalker; I can't wait to hear."

"Well, I had two good meetings today, both of which I believe resulted in small wins that will help people." Jim shares the details of his meeting with Priscilla.

"Why do you think you saw a different side to her today?" asks Prof-I.

"Well, after our meeting, she sent me an email, which gave me some insight. She felt supported during our meeting, which was different from her experience at the agency. She felt that no one took the work or challenges she and her team faced seriously and that her department wasn't a priority to others, including Rob. She is right. I also understand why she shuts down or negatively responds to others. We don't show her the respect earned by her experience and knowledge; she is always questioned. I plan to help her find her place and voice in the agency and will do my part to make her feel that she is a valued team member."

"Today was just the beginning. Your actions and your words will play a key role in facilitating that. People hear what you do, says Prof-I. I know it sounds weird, but others look for whether your actions match your words or your expectations of them. I am glad you're giving life to helping others become their best selves. Your convictions will pay dividends in leading others."

The two spend the next few minutes of the ride discussing Jim's schedule for the rest of the week and strategies for engaging his team, other divisions, and stakeholders. Prof-I pulls the cab into Jim's driveway.

"Door-to-door service today to celebrate your success."

"I am humbled and honored," replies Jim.

They exchange pleasantries and part ways. Jim greets his family with hugs and kisses.

"Daddy, I got an A on my science project."

"Good job, Ben. How about a ball game this weekend?" "Yes," Ben runs through the house, screaming!

Each member of the family recounts their day's events over dinner. At bedtime, Jim sleeps like a log.

Eager to begin his day, Jim is waiting outside for Prof-I to arrive. Without a minute to spare, Prof-I's cab pulls up.

"Morning, Jim, waiting for someone?" asks Prof-I.

"No one special," replies Jim with a smile.

He hops into the cab, and they head for the office. On the way, they discuss some of the successes and challenges Jim has encountered in his new role. They agree that he is gaining clarity regarding his convictions and having insights into himself as an individual. They both agree that Jim's journey in developing himself as a leader is just beginning. Prof-I wishes Jim a good day when they arrive at DCFS. Jim returns the sentiment.

"I'll be fine; I have no troubles in this world," responds Prof-I.

Jim looks at him quizzically, unsure what to make of Prof-I's statement.

When he enters his office, his Executive Assistant hands him files to review and reminds him of his nine o'clock meeting with his team. Before he can get settled, he hears them in the conference room. Jim greets his team and sits at the head of the conference table. He points to the newsprint on the wall on which he wrote his convictions and purpose. He reads his convictions aloud and explains how they support his purpose.

"I want you to take the next fifteen minutes to think about your convictions and purpose, share them, and let's see what we all have in common and how we can join forces to create our collective convictions and purpose. One of the first steps to becoming an effective team is to have some collective understanding of what we believe in and why we exist together."

"I thought we were meeting to continue our discussion on our division's initiatives and prioritize them," Ali responds.

"We'll get to that later. Besides, I'm still waiting on feedback from Rebecca on the issues I elevated to her."

"You told us you would have some answers for us today," responds Juan.

"I know, and we will get back to them. The initiatives are important. However, what's more important is for us to understand who we are together, what we stand for, and what it means to the rest of the system."

"It sounds mushy," replies Stacey, the IT director.

"I agree," but I need you to trust me and where I'm going with this."

The team spends the next two and a half hours discussing their convictions and collective purpose. Ali shares that fairness is fundamental to him.

"I come from a place where people were mistreated based on appearance. It's not a good feeling."

Juan believes that helping people solve problems is critical to their success. Stacey discusses her purpose of improving communities, and Priscilla believes she exists to ensure everyone has the same opportunities. Jim has managed to engage them, and their excitement is palpable. Before long, they arrive at their collective convictions and purpose based on their themes. They all agree that the Operations Division is the lifeline of the entire agency. Their success allows agency employees to have the resources, information, and capabilities to help families. The team believes they exist to serve, support, and help others fulfill their potential. Jim writes it on flipchart paper and posts it on the wall.

"I like it! It's simple, and it not only captures our convictions, but it also states our purpose succinctly," says Ali.

"It's easy to remember. "I've seen mission statements that are a page long.

No one pays attention to them, much less remember them," Priscilla adds.

They spend a few more minutes discussing the next steps and strategies for communicating the convictions and purpose to the rest of their staff for feedback and discussion. The meeting concludes with everyone feeling good about their accomplishment. Jim tells them there will be more sessions like the one they had today. Everyone nods in agreement and heads back to their area.

Back in his office, Jim reviews the budget for the entire division for the first time and identifies the funds he can move around to support the priorities that Rebecca signed off on thus far. Before his new role, there was never a need for a big-picture perspective. Some of the programs in the budget have been funded year after year with no tangible results. He plans to talk to Rebeca about his ideas for reallocating funds. He works through lunch reading Rob's old emails and reports. There are several initiatives that the agency invested in that never went beyond the planning phase. He makes a note of them for his next meeting with Rebecca. As the day ends, Jim responds to a few emails, packs his bag, and heads downstairs, where as expected, Prof-I is waiting.

"What's going on, man; how was your day?" asks Prof-I.

"Great! It is a new beginning for our team. We found our common ground today; it appears that we're all in this work for the same reason. Our collective conviction and purpose are to serve, support, and develop others. It was great hearing everyone talk about why they want to help others."

"How does identifying your collective convictions and purpose help your team?" asks Prof-I.

"I'm hoping that gaining clarity about convictions and our purpose will increase everyone's commitment and improve how we work within our team and collaborate with other divisions."

They continue to discuss Jim's work with his team and ways he can enhance his ability to lead them. Before long, they arrive at Jim's home. Jim thanks Prof-I for listening and guiding him.

"There's something about you that feels different. I can't quite figure it out yet," says Jim.

"When you do, please don't hesitate to share. It may help me better understand myself," Prof-I responds with self-deprecating laughter.

Jim exits the cab and walks toward his house. He turns around to wave goodnight to Prof-I, but to his surprise, he's already gone. *"Man, he's fast!"* he thinks as he opens the door. Before turning in for the night, he enjoys dinner and quality time with his family.

The following day, Jim arrives at work energized; the ride with Prof-I was enlightening, as usual. He spends the morning and early afternoon in and out of meetings, laying out some long-term plans and reallocating funds to different projects. As he turns to his computer, there's a knock on his door.

"Come in, please."

It's Stacey, the IT Director.

"Jim, do you have a few minutes?"

"Of course! I was about to send a few emails, but they can wait. What's going on?"

"It's my team. As you know, we have struggled to be responsive to our customers over the years. I just finished meeting with them, and I have to say, it was very disheartening."

"What made you feel that way?"

"Well, everyone seems to focus on themselves and insist that all the problems rest with the customers. It was a struggle to get them to take ownership for their part; there's much finger-pointing and blaming within the team," she explains.

"That must be frustrating for you," he empathizes.

"It's very frustrating; I have to be honest, there are days I don't want to show up for work."

"I'm sorry you experience those feelings. I've been there myself. How can I support you?"

"I'm not sure what I need. I just want them to take ownership of the work we do."

Jim pauses before responding.

"Remember our meeting yesterday when we reflected on our individual and collective convictions and purpose?

Stacy nods.

You shared that your purpose is to improve communities."

"I'm very clear and committed to my convictions and purpose," she

replies.

"Are they clear about theirs—individually and collectively?" She's silent for a moment.

"I'm not sure. How do I find out?

Jim resists the urge to respond and just sits there. After a moment of silence, Stacey answers her own question.

I need to ask them."

Jim smiles.

"What do your employees want for themselves, and why do they choose to do this work? Why do they choose to do it for this agency and the people we serve? Don't be alarmed if some people's responses focus on themselves and their needs. However, you will find that some staff members share a purpose similar to yours or are also here in service of the larger mission. Therefore, you need to ask questions."

Stacy shares her plan for engaging her team in conversations about their individual and collective purpose. She tells Jim that she plans to meet individually with her staff over the next few weeks and that she will also include this type of discussion in her managers' meetings and her upcoming all-staff meeting. She thanks Jim for listening and heads back to her unit.

Jim meets with Rebecca next to brief her on his week and his assessment of his division. He follows up on the list of priorities and initiatives and shares his thoughts about where they fit in the larger scheme of things and reallocating funds to support them. She asks a few questions but seems pleased with what Jim presented.

"How are people responding to you being in charge?"

"I think a better question might be, how am I responding to being in charge?

Rebecca looks at him, waiting for him to elaborate.

When you offered me this opportunity, I wasn't quite sure of myself or what you meant by 'turn things around.' Over the past several weeks, with the help of a good friend, I discovered what is important to me and what's important to the people you asked me to lead. Along the way, I landed on a leadership style that works for me and one that my team seems to respond to positively. They seem more energized than I've seen them in the past."

"Are they getting the work done?"

"They've always gotten the work done, but no one paid attention, appreciated their efforts, or asked for their input. They are a team of competent individuals who need the support, resources, and trust we have for other divisions. They are a team of leaders that will play a crucial role in moving our key initiatives along. In addition to getting the work done, I've watched this team interact with each other in a much more positive way. We got off to a rough start, but we are clicking now."

"What's different?"

Jim thinks for a moment before he responds.

"We realize that we are all here for the same reason." "What?" a confused Rebecca asks.

"We found things that we collectively believe in. I will share more later.

Jim glances at his watch.

I'm sorry, but I believe my cab is waiting."

"You take a cab?"

"It's a long story! I need to run."

"Okay, go ahead," responds Rebecca.

Jim rushes downstairs, jumps into the cab, and greets Prof-I.

"How's it going, Prof-I?"

"All is well, Jim. My day was splendid. "How was your day?"

"My day was remarkable," Jim replies and details his meetings with Stacey and Rebecca. He describes the difference in the team's energy, their interactions with each other, and how they were respectful and supportive.

"I'm not surprised, says Prof-I. You set the tone by being clear about your convictions and bringing them to life through your actions. This was the type of leadership they needed to experience. Was that their experience when Rob was at the helm?"

"Not that I recall. Rob was a nice guy, but I never knew what he stood for the more I think about it. He seemed to just go with the flow. We never seemed to commit to anything as a team. We just showed up every day and focused on our individual work."

As they pull in front of the house, Prof-I asks Jim to take the time to summarize his experiences from the week, then hands him a piece of paper.

"Just simple bullets; you don't have to write a dissertation."

Jim laughs as he exits the car. He walks to the driver's side and reaches for Prof-I's hand.

"Thank you," he says as he shakes Prof-I's hand.

Prof-I nods.

"Don't thank me yet. This was only the first leg of our journey. I'll see you next week."

As is his habit, Jim greets his family when he walks into the house. He never fails to remind them how much he loves them, not only with words but with hugs that would make an on-looker think they had been apart for days and not hours.

"Takeout Friday, I called it first," he says.

"Pizza Delight," Ben jumps and screams with joy.

Marcia is not as happy.

"We always have pizza; I want Thai food."

"We can have that as well," Jim replies.

Pam places the orders and sets the table.

After dinner, Jim takes some time to summarize his leadership experience.

He notes the following:

(1) To be an effective leader, one must look in the mirror and reflect on their life's journey to clarify their convictions and purpose.

(2) When a person is clear about their beliefs and what they stand for, and can bring them to life through their actions, it increases their credibility and their ability to influence others.

Jim knows he has embarked on an extraordinary journey; however, he also realizes that consistency and his ability to sustain his actions will be critical. He looks at the paper Prof-I gave him and reads it.

Start thinking about the leadership legacy you want to leave behind and live each day in service of your legacy like it's your last day on this earth.

"Hmm!" Jim murmurs as he turns off the lights and heads to bed.

Reflect and answer the following questions:

- Who are you?

- Why do you believe you exist? What is your purpose?

- What are your core beliefs and principles?

- Are you living your purpose? If not, why not? If yes, how?

- How are people responding to your leadership?

- Are you leading from a position of purpose versus a position of power and authority? Explain.

Chapter Four: Communicate the Direction

"Operate in the present while walking in the future."

Although Jim's weekend was filled with fun and laughter, it went by quickly. He and Ben caught a baseball game, the family went to the movies, and he and Pam did some work in the yard that they had been putting off for some time. Now it is the beginning of another week, and Jim is waiting for Prof-I. He is standing in the living room, staring out the window and feeling anxious. Jim knows that his team has a few critical deadlines to meet this week, and the anxiety persists despite his confidence that they will meet them.

Jim is startled out of his thoughts by the sound of a horn. *"Ah, Prof-I, right on time!"* Jim gets into the cab, and Prof-I greets him enthusiastically.

"Good morning, Jimbo. Are you ready to take another step in your journey?"

"I am not only ready to learn but also eager to put things into practice, Jim replies as they drive off. Before we begin our discussion, have you noticed that people stare when we drive by? Maybe it's just me, but it seems as if people look at me in the back seat a bit curiously. I'm almost tempted to wave at them."

"Feel free to do so. Maybe they think you are a celebrity."

"I may just do that one day," responds Jim.

"Okay, enough of the red-carpet stuff for one day. I have an important question I want you to think about this week. Where are you going, and where are you taking your team?

Jim is puzzled by the question.

Clarity of purpose is essential in leading, but it's only one leg of the journey. Successful leaders are also clear about their vision and can articulate it in a way that inspires others. Imagine going to work daily and tackling all the initiatives you've discussed but not being clear about how these things fit together or the end goal."

"I would feel disconnected," Jim replies.

"Not only would you feel disconnected, but you would also feel lost, Prof-I responds. It's challenging for leaders to help their followers connect to a common purpose without having a clear future direction."

"How do we clarify our direction?"

"Begin with your purpose, which you have done. It's like a journey within your journey. Once you are clear about your purpose, you must envision your destination."

They pull up to the building.

"You've certainly given me food for thought. I'm excited about where we are as a team; I just feel like we are marching in place. We need to be moving forward."

"Moving forward to where? That is the question you need to answer for yourself and your team."

Jim exits the cab and heads into the building with that question in mind.

Jim participates in meetings, planning sessions, and daily project briefings. In most instances, he finds himself proposing solutions that will improve a situation or make people's lives better. The remainder of the week follows a similar pattern; he feels that people are positively responding to him and his team. They've even managed to start repairing damaged relationships with other divisions. He overhears someone from another division talking about their positive experience with Priscilla's team.

"It was as if they cared," the woman shares with her colleagues.

It's late on Friday, and Jim scribbles a few notes summarizing the week's interactions. He noted how he and his team served, supported, and helped others in their development. Jim feels they are gaining traction by adhering to their collective purpose.

When he arrives downstairs, Prof-I is waiting, as usual. Jim gets in, and they exchange greetings.

"How was your day, Jim?"

"Fine, and yours?"

"No problem, mon. The day is the day. It comes, and it goes. I just do my little part in the universe."

Surprisingly, Jim responds,

"That's all we can do, brother."

Prof-I turns and looks at him.

"Are you getting spiritual on me, brethren?"

"Maybe. It all came full circle today. I took your advice, reflected on our purpose, and paid attention to my interactions with others throughout the day. For example, Lori, one of the managers from another division, appeared to be struggling with adjusting to the culture and rhythm of the agency. I met with her this afternoon and helped her think differently about her role and career. At the end of our conversation, she was in a much better frame of mind."

"What did you do?" asks Prof-I.

"Listened, asked questions, and shared some common experiences. Anyway, at the end of the conversation, she identified ways she could add value to her division and the agency. I agreed to mentor her. More importantly, I gave her examples of how I live my convictions and purpose at work and in my personal life. This seemed to resonate with her, and she glowed when talking about her purpose."

"It sounds like you are finding your way along this journey. How does it feel?"

"Energizing!" I'm still struggling with being clear about where we are going or our ideal future state as a team."

"What do you find challenging about it?"

Jim pauses for a minute and then responds.

"The moment I get to work, I am inundated with issues, emails, meetings, and fighting fires related to what's happening that day. It's difficult to think about what I want to do tomorrow or next week. It's a stretch to think about what I should be doing a year or three to five years from now."

"I agree. The days' events are enough to keep us occupied, and they consume most of our limited time on our schedules, Prof-I asserts.

However, if we stay on the hamster wheel, we are not only maintaining the status quo for ourselves but also doing the same for our team and our organizations. Charting a direction with an exciting vision and goals energizes people and allows them to imagine possibilities and engage in innovative conversations. It may be difficult for your managers to stay connected to your purpose without a sense of where you are trying to go."

"Whenever we talk, I feel like you know what I need to do; why don't you just tell me and make it easier for both of us."

"That's not how it works, responds Prof-I. There are no quick fixes to the challenges people face. My role is to serve as a sounding board and to engage you. The reflection and thinking are on you. You should be doing this when you engage with those you lead. Giving someone all the answers does not help them develop; instead, you are enabling their incompetence and dependency. We all need to become critical thinkers! However, I will share this, charting a clear direction is not something you do in passing.

You must make time for it and create a space that allows your team to participate."

Jim does not respond. He jots down a few notes before they arrive at his home.

"Thank you, Prof-I, it has been an enlightening journey, as always. Have a good evening".

Over the next week, Jim facilitates a series of 'visioning sessions' with his leadership team, where each of them discusses their commitment to the work of the agency and its clients. During one of the sessions, Jim recalls Priscilla's statements about the importance of recruiting and hiring the right people.

"We cannot put the lives of kids and families in the hands of just anyone who needs a job. We need to do a better job of screening and interviewing."

"It is important to have a sound learning and development infra-structure; this will lead to innovative service delivery practices," says Ali.

"It's critical that my team gets the tools needed to do their jobs," Juan interjects.

"There is a need to deploy new technologies to help employees be more efficient in their roles," suggests Stacey.

After several meetings, they arrive at their long-term direction. Jim writes on the whiteboard:

"An innovative system of care in which everyone has the resources to partner with others to serve communities, children, and families."

This is their big-picture vision for the Operations Division. The team takes a few minutes to discuss what it means for the division and their respective units. Everyone is on board with this new energizing vision. Next, they explore strategies for sharing it with their staff.

"I suggest we hold off until we have developed tangible goals to support it. Maybe we could review our priorities and determine how they align with our vision."

"That's a great idea, Stacey; I'll send you the agency's goals that Rebecca shared at the last executive management team meeting. Our vision is very much in line with those goals," Jim says as the meeting ends. The team is feeling energized and enthused. They discuss this side of Jim, one they have never seen before, his new role. It's as if he was invisible when he reported to Rob.

The following week, Jim and Prof-I discuss his success in clarifying his purpose and helping his team define its collective purpose and vision.

"We plan to spend time reviewing our priorities and establishing the broad goals we want to pursue and accomplish over the next three years. This will help us to determine where we want to expend our energy and invest our resources. These goals will also bring our vision to life and help us determine if we are successful."

"I think that's great! My only advice is to keep the goals broad—at the 10,000 feet level, Prof-I suggests. Keeping the goals broad allows the people who need to operationalize them to explore various options related to their work. Also, remember that one of the challenges a leader faces is to contemplate the future while fighting fires in the present."

There is a lull in the conversation as Jim thinks about how most of his meetings with Rebecca and the executive management team are about putting out today's fires, leaving little time for imagining what's possible. As Prof-I pulls up to his house, Jim shares his thoughts.

"My vision is exactly what I would like for those who need the assistance of DCFS. I am often frustrated with the bureaucracy that sometimes gets in the way of serving communities, families, and children. Some of the red tape that internal and external customers go through to get what they need is ridiculous and often unnecessary. When my grandmother needed the government's help, the process often felt invasive, ridiculing, and non-responsive. We felt like a case number rather than a family that needed help. I don't want that for the families we serve. I want them to be successful and for our agency to be supportive, not one that creates barriers."

Jim spends the time that evening reflecting on what he said to Prof-I. After processing his thoughts, he notes how his perception of serving families aligns with the vision he and his team share. This is the utopian state for the work we do. I know this is possible with the right people and the willingness to do things differently.

Being able to define and articulate what he would like the agency's future to be, lifts a weight that Jim was unaware he was carrying and allows him to enjoy the rest of his weekend with his family.

Riding to work on Monday morning, Jim notices people staring and pointing at the cab.

"They're doing it again," he says, staring through the window.

"Maybe it's the ads on the cab, replies Prof-I. Some of them are very intriguing."

Excited about his vision for the future, Jim changes the subject and shares some additional thoughts about his team's common vision.

What does it mean?" asks Prof-I.

"It means that if we hire the right people, ensure they have all the tools and resources they need to support children and families, and support them the same way we expect them to support the families they serve, our vision will be realized."

"Sounds very utopian."

"But worth striving for!" Jim states adamantly.

"Your challenge is not to convince me. It's to persuade the people who do the work that this vision is something they should want to strive for or be a part of."

Upon arriving at his office, Jim is bombarded with a slew of telephone messages, most notably one from Rebecca. She has rescheduled their 9:00 a.m. meeting for 1:15 p.m. *Well, that's just great!* After putting away his belongings, he calls his Executive Assistant.

"Marie, please round up the management team. Tell them we will meet at 10:00, plan for a three-hour meeting, and cancel everything else except for my meeting with Rebecca."

The team arrives in the conference room at 10:00, feeling rushed and looking puzzled. Jim quickly reassures them.

"No need to be alarmed; no one is in trouble. This is short notice, but this will be a good meeting. I want us to spend the rest of the morning discussing our division's future, how it aligns with our shared vision, and how we plan to achieve it."

Everyone looks around the room at each other. Jim can see that they are willing but somewhat hesitant, so he kicks things off by once again writing on the whiteboard.

An innovative system of care in which everyone has the resources to partner with others to serve communities, children, and families.

Seeing the vision written in large print resonates with the team.

"Does anyone have any questions?"

Juan is the first to speak.

"Do you think this is possible?"

"Not only do I believe it's possible, but I'm also committed to doing my part, which is what I'm asking of you," responds Jim.

"I can buy into it; I'm just not sure everyone in my area will. People come to work to do their jobs and go home to their families at the end of the day. This may seem too philosophical to them."

"That's where we come in, Priscilla chimes in. Our job is to help our employees connect what they do daily to something greater than their individual work. Two of the questions I constantly get from my HR staff are 'where is the agency heading' and 'what are we trying to achieve?' I believe that in a sense, our employees are asking for guidance and, to some extent, a vision."

"Shouldn't we be clear on the agency's vision?" asks Stacey.

"Yes, we should, but, at this time, an agency vision has not been precisely defined or communicated. That shouldn't prevent us from moving forward with our vision. As long as it aligns with the agency's mission, we'll all be on the same page, responds Jim. I will discuss the agency's vision with Rebecca to better understand what that is."

Over the next two hours, the team works with Jim to review their priorities and identify four broad goals:

1. improve internal customer service

2. improve operational efficiency

3. equip staff with the best available resources

4. cultivate a culture of learning

"Aren't these goals too broad?" asks Ali.

"They are! We shouldn't address the weeds at this level. We want our goals to be broad enough to allow you and your team to think about the various ways you can make them happen. This is where the conversations, creativity, and innovation come into play," Jim explains.

"In other words, we own the weeds," Stacy chimes in.

"Exactly!" responds Priscilla.

"Man! I get excited just thinking about the different ways we can support people's learning and development in the agency. We are so wedded to traditional classroom practices. I often ask myself, are we promoting learning or training?" Ali shares.

After discussing the goals, the team agrees and begins to explore ways to share them with staff and respond to questions and concerns that may arise. They all agree that the process and buy-in will be a marathon, not a sprint. The staff will need time to get used to thinking and behaving in a way that supports the division's mission, vision, and goals. Once we roll all this out, people will better understand where we are going and what we are trying to accomplish. A big part of our role is to help them figure out how they can help us get there," suggests Jim.

With a sense of accomplishment, the team wraps up the meeting. Sitting alone in the conference room, Jim reflects on the progress they continue to make collectively. *"They have gelled and are supportive of each other."* He uses this rare moment of quiet to make mental notes about his approach to helping his team get on track. Realizing that they lacked clarity and direction under Rob's leadership and spent most of their time responding to fires and playing catch up is glaring. The ringing of the phone interrupts his thoughts.

"Hello, this is Jim; how can I help you?"

"Jim, it's Marie; you have five minutes before your meeting with Rebecca."

"Thanks, I'm on my way, and Marie, I'll be leaving for the day following the meeting."

Before Jim can leave the conference room, there's a knock, and the door opens.

"Rebecca! Jim says in a startled voice; I was just on my way to you."

"No need; I thought I would come to you since I was in the area. I have a couple of agenda items; do you have anything you want to discuss?"

"I have some resource needs, and I want to update you on how things are going with my division."

"Okay then, let's get started."

Rebecca shares that some changes are coming down the pike. Many will affect Jim's division. For example, the new child safety laws will require changes to the IT system and training of 1,200 existing employees and modifications to the training for new employees and contract staff.

"As you can see, your division will play a key role in ensuring these initiatives are successful," Rebecca concluded.

"This is a great segue into my discussion about resources. The staff development team has done a remarkable job responding to the increased demands for system-wide training. However, we are burning them out. Many of them are in the classroom three to five days a week. I need to bring on two more developers to meet deadlines on two key IT projects. The state mandates one, and the other is implementing our new case-management system." After some discussion and clarity about expectations, Rebecca agrees to give Jim additional resources. He spends the next few minutes updating her on his team's progress.

"How's Priscilla adjusting to the changes?" asks Rebecca.

"She is contributing immensely," he replies.

"I am happy to hear that. I understand she can be difficult."

"That's not been my experience with her. She has been a pleasure to work with."

Rebecca pauses, then asks.

"What have you done to get her to that point?"

"She wants what many of us want from our work environment— to feel valued."

Rebecca looks at Jim but does not respond. They wrap up the meeting by summarizing their agreements and confirming his role and support for the upcoming changes.

Grabbing his belongings, Jim rushes to meet Prof-I. During the journey, they discuss Jim's success in clarifying the direction in which he is leading his team.

"How will you determine if you and the team are on course or if you need to adjust?" Prof-I asks.

"I plan to use our vision, mission, and goals as the focus of our weekly leadership meetings. Each leader will be asked to share what they are doing to support our agreed direction. They are also free to share their successes, challenges, and the support they need. They'll be some repetitions as I may do check-ins during biweekly one-to-ones with my team. Essentially, it's their meeting. I'll be there to listen, ask questions, and lend my support," Jim shares.

"How will you and the team deal with accountability?" asks Prof-I.

"I'm not sure what you mean."

"What happens if someone does not actively support the direction of the division?

Jim pauses. He hadn't given that scenario much thought; he assumed that people would do their part and stay on track with the direction the team agreed to pursue.

Your managers must own the vision and goals you collectively agreed to. It should also be expected that their success or failure in achieving these goals will reflect their performance. Therefore, the goals should be included in their expectations and will require difficult conversations if someone fails to deliver on their end, explains Prof-I. Are you comfortable with having those conversations? He continues.

Jim says nothing; however, he nods in agreement as he gives the idea some thought.

It's not as simple as a handshake when it comes to accountability. Ownership is the first piece of the accountability puzzle; next must be the expectation that you will provide details of your actions and commitment. Accountability is often ignored when it comes to leading people. Sometimes leaders hope and pray that people will stay on course or do their part. That's not always the case. Self and team accountability must be included in the process."

Due to heavy traffic, they arrive at Jim's house a little later than usual. Goodbyes are exchanged, and Prof-I drives off. Jim heads inside, his head buzzing with Prof-I's words. Jim has dinner with his family, inquiring about their day. Mentally exhausted, he goes to bed early.

The following day, he is waiting outside for Prof-I, who arrives shortly after 7 a.m. After greeting each other, they pick up the conversation where they left off the day before. Prof-I shares some ideas about accountability:

- Re-verify that everyone is on board with the direction you agreed upon

- Ask team members to share their plans for achieving the shared goals

- Incorporate the goals into team members' performance expectations

- Create a space/opportunity for regular check-ins in which team members share their successes, challenges, and needs

- Have difficult conversations focusing on the gap between what's expected and what is delivered.

- Offer support to help the person close the gap

After Prof-I shares his ideas Jim responds,

"I'm clear about everything you have suggested except the last one. Tell me more about having difficult conversations that focus on the gap. What does that mean?"

After a moment, Prof-I expounds.

"They're called difficult conversations because they are just that. They are difficult. Leaders tend to shy away from them for several reasons. When they do have them, it's out of frustration or comes from a place of emotions and often misses the mark. The focus of the conversation must be on what the person has failed to do or deliver compared to what you expected; then, it is about performance, observations, and results. Not your feelings about the person."

Jim mulls over conversations with his team members and how emotions and frustration drove the dialog.

"I must admit that when I've had difficult conversations, they have not gone well. And in some instances, the person walks away disheartened and with little clarity about what I expected from them. This is very insightful!"

They continue the discussion and end by summarizing the leadership process of clarifying and communicating the team's direction as follows:

- Defining the purpose
- Articulating the vision
- Setting clear goals
- Encouraging self and team accountability

During the discussion, Jim again notices people pointing at the cab. He rolls the window down and yells.

"Can I help you?"

People react by placing their hands over their mouths and staring.

"What's with those people?"

"Why do you ask?" Prof-I responds calmly.

"Haven't you noticed how people stare and point at the cab when we drive by?"

"No, I haven't. I try to keep my eyes on the road. It's safer and keeps my insurance premium low.

Jim sighs in frustration.

About your team's direction, I think you should spend one more meeting summarizing your division's direction, the way we did this morning."

"I agree. I will also share my plans for keeping everything on our radar."

They pull up in front of the building. As Jim gets out, Prof-I wishes him well and leaves.

In the office, Jim notes how the team can hold each other accountable and monitor performance, finishing just in time for his weekly leadership meeting. He walks into the conference room to find the team waiting and thinks about how different things were from the first couple of sessions when they were late and unprepared.

"Thanks for coming. Now, what's new, what's challenging, and how can the rest of us support you?"

The team is quiet at first, then Stacey jumps in.

"The two servers we ordered came in yesterday: we'll be installing them tonight. So, if you have people working past 5 p.m., they will not have access to the system. But when everyone comes into work in the morning, they should notice that the system is much faster."

"Thanks, Stacey. What do you need from us?"

"Just give staff the heads up."

Jim was about to ask Stacey to draft an email, which he would review before it was sent to the staff. He catches himself and pauses.

"Stacey, why don't you send out the email? I don't need to review it."

She's a bit taken aback. Rob, their previous director, always sent out the emails that went to the entire agency. Stacy smiles.

"I'll take care of it as soon as I get back to my office."

"I don't know if this is new or exciting, but today is my thirtieth anniversary with this agency, Juan shares.

There is a round of applause and congratulations.

I just want to thank Jim for what we've been doing lately: meeting, defining our purpose, goals, and all that stuff. My time here would have been much easier if someone had helped me focus on my team's work. I feel like I'm part of a team now."

"Thanks, Juan, but just to let you all know, there's more to come."

Priscilla and Ali state that they have nothing to add but pledge to support their colleagues. Jim hands out copies of his summary of the team's purpose, vision, and goals, allowing everyone a few minutes to read it.

"Please feel free to ask any questions or share your thoughts," he says.

"Is it okay if I share something I worked on with my unit? Asks Priscilla.

She hands out a document that lists HR goals and strategies that support the larger division's goals.

I took what we've been working on and duplicated the process with my team. It has helped us clarify our role and prioritize the initiatives and projects we need to work on."

Everyone is impressed.

"Priscilla, this is great and a perfect segue into what I want to discuss. You must collaborate with your managers to help them align their work with what we have laid out here. We will only succeed if everyone is aligned, feels valued, and understands how they contribute to our collective success. Does anyone have any questions?"

"What happens if we don't meet our goals?" asks Ali.

Jim pauses before responding,

"If there are legitimate reasons, like lack of resources, shifts in priorities, etc., then we will adjust. However, if goals are not met because of a lack of effort or your leadership ineffectively supports the bigger picture, we need to discuss accountability. This is vastly different from how we've operated in the past. Change the mindset and practice, and you change the culture. I want us to build a culture of innovation and accountability, and for us to accomplish that, I will need your input and commitment. Let's do this together! We could be the example for the other divisions."

There is a moment of silence, then,

"I'm on board. My only request is that we support each other in ways that we haven't in the past. If I ask for help, I need it. I am willing to sacrifice my own needs at times if it benefits the team. I hope everyone else is willing to do the same," Priscilla says.

"Count me in, as long as I don't have to listen to Ali's long-winded philosophical stories," Juan says with a smile.

"It's about history and context, man. You can't move forward without having the right perspective. For example . . ."

"Not now, Ali, we don't have time," everyone says in unison.

"I was just going to say . . ."

"Ali, can you get to the point, please," Jim interrupts.

Ali smiles and relents. Jim closes the meeting by confirming his next one-on-one session with each leader. He also reminds them that their status reports are due in two weeks, and they should include where they are with implementing the goals within their respective units.

Jim spends the remainder of the day in his office. He notes that a few contracts underspent this fiscal year, knowing that they could be potential sources for paying for other services at the end of the year.

Jim knows tomorrow will be a significant day at the executive leadership team meeting with Rebecca to discuss system-wide changes and critical initiatives. Wanting to have all his focus there, he ends his day sending and responding to time-sensitive emails.

Downstairs, he finds Prof-I waiting in the lobby.

"This is the first time I've seen you out of your cab. Is everything okay?"

"I just wanted to see what the inside of your playground looks like."
"Playground?" Jim questions with a half-smile.

"Work is play, play is work, if you enjoy what you do," Prof-I explains.

Jim's smile widens. On their way to the car, Jim updates Prof-I on his efforts around clarifying and communicating a direction for his division.

"You've accomplished a lot since we met. You should begin to see the fruits of you sowing the few seeds of leadership we've discussed so far. Do you still feel like a boss in charge?"

"What do you mean?"

"When I met you, you were very certain that your team should do as you say simply because you were given a new title and some power. Over the past few months, I get the sense that you have taken a different approach."

"I see things differently now, responds Jim as they begin their journey. The team has responded well to being included in setting the direction and creating a different culture for our division. When Rob was our manager, I felt that people just looked forward to the end of the day. Our day-to-day operation was drone-like. Thanks to the team, we are re-energized and have clarity on where we want to go and how to get there. I want to thank you for coaching me on becoming a better leader. I was a bit skeptical initially, but what I have learned during our time together has paid dividends in moving people who appeared to be stuck, including myself."

"No need to thank me, my role in life is to help to create a better world through others. The key to doing so lies in our willingness to build relationships. That is a critical lesson on leadership. I had to earn your trust, and you had to earn the trust of your team, which I believe you have done. But I must caution you; losing people's trust only takes one slip. So, make sure you continue practicing what you ask of them. If you are unwilling to do something, don't make it a requirement for others."

Jim is in a daze as he gets out of the cab and walks into his house. He knows that he, his team, and the agency will face some tough challenges, but he feels better prepared to deal with them.

Key Leadership Actions for Clarifying and Communicating Direction

- Work with your team to define its collective purpose and mission. Help team members align their collective purpose with the organization's mission and vision.

- Partner with your team to discover a vision that speaks to your collective aspirations.

- Agree on core principles that will guide the work and the team's engagement.

- Help individuals of the team to align their core principles with the team's collective principles.

- Review the organization's priorities and use them to define your team's priorities.

- Help team members align their work with the team's collective priorities. In essence, you are asking them to think about how they will contribute to the team's collective success.

- Ensure individual and collective accountability by practicing everything you created above.

Chapter Five: Courageously Confront Change

"Courageous leadership will test the tides of change while unlocking untapped ideas, talent, and innovation in the face of change and uncertainty."

The next day, Jim is summoned to an emergency meeting with Rebecca and the executive team.

"The mayor is concerned about the pandemic as the number of new cases is increasing in the city. He is talking about a potential shutdown!" Rebecca exclaims.

The questions come quickly as everyone panics.

"What are we supposed to do?"

"How will we serve our clients?"

"How will our staff do their jobs?"

Rebecca's annoyance is evident; she's about to pull the plug on the meeting when Jim speaks up.

"Look, I know this will be tough, but we developed a contingency plan with a virtual work component a few years ago. This may be a suitable time to put it to use."

There is silence; then Matt, the CFO, voices his concerns about the potential costs to the agency for allowing people to work from home. The others echo the sentiment. Marilyn from Contracts is concerned about the timing.

"We are in the middle of conforming contracts. We need people working in the office. Contracts can't be processed unless we are physically here. The computer system, the files, everything we need is in this building!" she exclaims.

"This shutdown is going to happen whether we are prepared or not! We can spend this time pointing out all the things that won't work, or we can prepare for dealing with the inevitable," Jim asserts.

Rebecca, about to stop Jim, is impressed by his take-charge attitude. Jim agrees to collaborate with his colleagues to help them implement their plans for their divisions. He schedules meetings with each division director over the next week. The meeting adjourns with the anxiety level of the executive team lowered just a notch.

Jim returns to his office and calls an impromptu meeting with his team. He shares the information from the executive team meeting and allows the team to share their thoughts and concerns.

"Look at how we have grown individually and as a team over the past few months. We've overcome some tremendous challenges; this is yet another challenge. The magnitude of what is being asked of us is unprecedented, but if we work together as we have lately, we will be fine. We've been clear about our direction, and our flexibility has allowed us to adapt in the face of adversity. Our staff has responded favorably to our leadership, and many have stepped up to the leadership plate themselves. We can do this."

Ali shares his concerns about his team losing the ability to deliver in-person training. With Jim's guidance, he thinks about how he can use various technologies to support staff learning.

"It will take time for my team and participants to get comfortable with this approach, but we will make it work," Ali responds confidently.

"I'm a little anxious, Jim; much of the heavy lifting for transitioning to virtual work will fall on my team," Stacey, the IT director, admits.

"Why don't you assess the current state of the agency's technology capabilities and determine what needs to be done to support the other divisions. Rebecca has stated that we will have the flexibility to purchase new technologies and equipment needed to make this work," he shares.

"Okay, my team and I can pull something together in about two days for your review."

"That will be great, Stacy. I would like all of you to be a part of my meetings with the division directors and their leadership teams. You will be able to hear from them directly and help to inform their plans. In the meantime, I expect each of you to convene huddles with your staff to listen to their concerns, get their input, and share your ideas.

The team smiles in unison.

Why are you guys smiling?" Jim asks.

"We were just texting each other that we need to do what was asked of us," Priscilla responds.

Jim smiles and thanks them for their leadership.

"While most of our team will work virtually full time, I plan to be on-site at least two to three days a week. I'm not asking you to do the same, but I want to be onsite until the system gets comfortable working remotely."

Ali, head of Staff Development, chimes in without hesitation,

"I'm planning to be onsite as well. Based on our roles, our team will be the lifeline for everyone else during the change; therefore, we must have a strong presence."

Everyone else shares the same conviction. They close the meeting and commit to communicating with each other regularly as they plan for the transition. Before they leave, Jim has one final message,

"This is a challenge we can face and conquer!"

Far more confident in their abilities, they disperse to meet with their staff immediately.

Jim meets with Marie, his executive assistant, and informs her of the department's plan to implement virtual working in response to the pandemic. He asks her to think about what she will need to work remotely. They work together to schedule two-hour blocks of time to work with other divisions over the next week. Having thanked Marie for her help, Jim reviews the staffing and functions of each division in preparation for his meetings with them. Before wrapping up for the day, he notes areas where he needs clarity.

When Jim arrives downstairs, the ever-punctual Prof-I is waiting. They exchange greetings as Jim climbs into the cab. He breathes a loud sigh of relief and lays his head on the headrest.

"It appears you have had a tough day," suggests Prof-I.

"Not really," I would say that it was eventful. We have quite a few tough decisions over the next two weeks, but I'm confident we'll be fine."

"Are you talking about the pending shutdown and the need for staff to work from home?"

"How do you know that?"

"I have my sources. That's one of the benefits of driving a cab; people tell you things."

Jim shares the details of his meetings with Prof-I.

"It sounds like they are looking to you for leadership. Why do you think that is the case?"

"I haven't given that much thought," Jim responds.

"When facing change and uncertainty, people need to hear a voice of optimism, someone who makes them feel safe and that success is possible. People also need clarity during change. While it's not always possible to be clear during change and uncertainty, they need to have a sense of direction.

This helps them think about their roadmap for success. One of the things I heard from you is that you created space for your team to provide input about a change that also affects them. This is critical. It makes them feel like they are making the change happen instead of the change simply happening to them. It's a different mindset."

"It just felt like it was what needed to be done at that moment. I've learned much about myself over the last several months from our journeys together. I've also been observing others lead and have seen the good, the bad, and even the ugly side of leadership. I made quite a few mental notes about lessons learned."

"Much of what you described are the result of seeds you planted. People have watched you lead and are encouraged about their abilities to influence change in the organization. Great leadership is not only impactful but also infectious," Prof-I summarizes.

Over the next several days, Jim and his team meet with other divisions to create a virtual work plan, allowing the agency to continue serving the needs of children and families during the shutdown. They partner with the deputies in the other divisions to present an agency-wide plan to the executive leadership team. During the presentation, they field some tough questions.

"Will our IT system handle the strain of increased remote work?"

Jim is calm but direct.

"We upgraded much of the hardware and software to allow more people to access our system externally. We also purchased and will distribute new laptops with more memory and speed. All laptops now have cameras, which will enable viewing during virtual meetings. So, dress appropriately, he says with a smile.

Jim fields a few more questions and reminds everyone that this is not an issue of choice.

We have to do this to ensure we continue to fulfill our mission during these times of uncertainty. There are no guarantees, but we need to be responsive and learn as we go."

Rebecca and the executive team review and discuss the plan before signing off.

Jim leaves the meeting satisfied. He is confident about his team's ability to support the agency during the transition to working from home. Jim heads to his conference room to meet his team. He relays the salient details about the executive team meeting, and they agree to work through lunch to adjust their plans and finalize the larger agency plan.

"It appears that you have earned Rebecca's trust," Priscilla shares.

"We all have. Our team has stepped up over the past year; your collective commitment to our vision and goals has paid dividends for us and the entire agency."

They wrap up the session and call it a day.

During the ride home, Jim shares the highlights from his meetings and discusses the executive leadership team's concerns and initial reluctance, despite having no choice but to act.

"People become comfortable with the headache they know and don't often muster the courage to change their condition. It's almost as if they are paralyzed by fear . . . the fear of failure, loss of their jobs or status, or even fear of success."

"Why would a leader fear success?" asks Jim.

"Success can result in change, which means people have to do things differently, or it may result in more work. For example, suppose you successfully implement and execute the plan. In that case, you will remove many of the other divisions' excuses for not allowing people to work remotely over the years. When the city reopens, it may choose to keep many of the processes you are implementing in place for the foreseeable future."

Jim recalls the number of times he has pushed for the executive team to implement remote work over the years and the pushback he received. The cab pulls up in front of his house. He gets out and walks around to the driver's side.

"I don't think you realize how much you've helped me transition into this leadership role," he says.

Prof-I is silent for a minute, then he responds,

"You have always had it in you; all you needed was support, guidance, and the confidence to lead."

"Thank you for helping me with those things. I took a risk challenging the executive team; in the past, I would have joined them in resisting change and maintaining the status quo."

"Well, I can't teach you courage, but I will say it requires the willingness to lose everything to do what you believe is right and necessary. You cannot worry about losing your job or the political ramifications of challenging the status quo. In some cases, death is the price you must be prepared to pay. That is one of the attributes of a great leader. Consider individuals like Martin Luther King, Jr., Thomas Paine, Alexander Hamilton, Malcolm X, Harvey Milk, and Emily Davison, to name a few. They died while leading others to do what was right or necessary. Are you willing to die for doing what's right, Jim?"

By Jim's facial expression, Prof-I could see that he was pondering this fundamental question. He wishes him a good evening, and Jim returns the sentiment in a distracted manner.

Jim enters the house and greets his family, with Prof-I's question at the back of his mind. Pam notices an undefinable change in her husband and mentions it before bedtime. Although tired, Jim talks excitedly about the encouragement he has been getting from Prof-I, how that has translated into his supporting his team, and the difference it's made in their attitudes and work.

The following day. Jim and Prof-I continue discussing Jim's success in getting the executive leadership team to support the pandemic work plan.

"This was a big win for you and your team; now you must deliver."

"We will. Today I will work with the executive leadership team to create a communications plan to ensure that everyone in the agency knows what they need to do and how they will be supported while working from home. We've already done some of the communication legwork in my division. We just need to make certain the rest of the agency is well informed, feel able to ask questions, and confidently contribute to the change. You taught me that the more you include people in change, the more they feel valued and engaged. This goes a long way in ensuring that we are collectively successful."

Arriving at the office, Jim wishes Prof-I 'a great day' and heads inside. He knows the decisions he makes over the next few weeks will be critical to the agency's success. However, Jim feels comfort in knowing that he has the right team to partner with to get things done.

Key Leadership Actions for Confronting Change

- Pay attention to your eco-system and your internal and external operating environment.

- Scan your ecosystem and identify significant shifts or events that are happening.

- Work with others to determine how they affect your work and your team or organization.

Key Leadership Actions for Confronting Change

- Identify the skills, resources, technology, etc., you currently have that will allow you to manage or take advantage of these shifts or events.

- Identify what's lacking within you, your team, or your organization that will impede your ability to deal with these shifts or changes effectively. Develop strategies for addressing these gaps.

- Craft consistent messaging informing people about:
  - Why you need to change
  - What will change and what will remain the same
  - How they can become involved in the change
  - Include messages of hope and provide a picture of what success looks like
- Create a space to allow others to share their fears and concerns about the change and provide input for successfully making the shift.

Chapter Six: Commission Others to Support the Mission and Vision

"You don't manage talent; you unleash it and enjoy the innovative changes that happen."

The past several months have been a critical turning point for Jim and his team, and this is the focus of their conversation this morning.

"You said something when we first met that resonated with me, says Jim. You reminded me that I could not get things done by myself. Effective leaders get things done through others, and as a result of changing the way I lead, I feel like I'm not working as hard as I did in the past. I don't attend as many meetings, and I'm approving more plans than I create."

"What are you doing differently?" asks Prof-I.

"I trust my team to get things done and don't feel the need to attend their project meetings, participate in every decision they make, or micro-manage everything in which they are involved. This is because we share the same mission, vision, and values and are all on the same page regarding our priorities. I ensure that I am available when they need my support. Some leaders may feel this is too much of a hands-off approach to leadership, but I beg to differ. We still plan together; I share my expectations and have regular check-ins, but they are empowered to lead. I've supported their development, enabling them to find their leadership voice and presence."

"Why do you think more managers don't do this?"

"That's an interesting question. I am sure there are many reasons, but I'll name a few based on how I was before I met you. As leaders, we misunderstand what it means to lead. Some of us may interpret leadership as being in charge, controlling the work, telling people what to do, and being in the fray of the day-to-day. I was able to flip the switch and change my leadership mindset to one of trusting, developing, coaching, empowering, and supporting. As you can see, it has paid dividends for me in my professional and personal lives."

"It sounds like you have delegated and encouraged, allowing others to use their knowledge, skills, and expertise to drive change and improve performance. An employee is only capable of doing what they are empowered to do. Once they are trusted to use their knowledge and skills, they become energized to act in support of the mission and vision."

The conversation concludes as they pull up in front of Jim's building.

Upon entering his office, Jim asks Marie to print out a list of his meetings for the week. Reviewing the schedule, he notices that many meetings include one or more leaders from his team. One example is the IT meeting tomorrow, which he and Stacey are scheduled to attend, while later in the day, he is to participate in a training meeting along with Ali. All his team members are meeting with other divisions about the remote work plan. Jim spends the next twenty minutes reviewing the schedule and deleting several meetings. He receives a slew of emails and phone calls from members of his leadership team inquiring about his absence from some of their meetings. They are taken aback by his response:

"You've got it; keep me posted."

He spends the rest of the week aligning his priorities with the agency's pandemic work plan.

Jim finds himself feeling less stressed and more productive. He spends more time coaching his staff, learning more about their plans, their successes, and the challenges they face. He also gains more clarity on how he can support them. Initially, Jim's team members were surprised by his reduced involvement in their work. They have since embraced his approach and have begun to emulate it with staff members who report directly to them. Because of this, everyone is engaged, there is less guesswork about who is responsible for what, and everybody is aware of what's happening. Consequently, the division's morale is higher than ever; it no longer feels like the one led by Rob.

The next day, Jim sits in his conference room, reviewing his budget, when Juan walks in.

"Hey Jim, we need to talk. I know you want us to turn more of the day-to-day work over to our staff and focus more on planning and leading, but some of my staff are not developed in certain areas."

"Thank you for sharing this with me. How can we address their skills gap?" asks Jim.

"What do you mean?"

"We shouldn't just write people off. We must explore all options in helping them develop their full potential."

"I don't have time! My plate is full. Between working on projects, writing reports, attending meetings, and my routine tasks, I don't have time to develop people."

"You are caught in one of those leadership conundrums," suggests Jim.

"What does that mean?" Jim pauses, then responds.

"Your plate is full because your team does not have the capabilities to do the things you need, but they are not skilled in certain areas because you don't have the time to focus on their development?"

"You've pretty much summed it up," Juan agrees.

"How much longer can you afford to continue that cycle?

He continues before Juan responds,

Your role as a leader is to get things done by enlisting and partnering with your staff. To do so, you must invest time in understanding their strengths and helping them develop their capabilities. Some may require training; others may need modeling and coaching on higher-level things such as relationship building, problem-solving, etc."

"I don't disagree with you, Jim, but where do I begin?"

"Let's spend some time during the shutdown focused on how we can develop our people. I think working from home will allow us to do things differently in this area," Jim suggests.

During the week, Jim and his team work with the various divisions to transition their staff to virtual work status. As they wrap things up on the last day of everyone working from the office, they discuss how many people were involved at all levels and share their excitement about the partnerships they have developed with other divisions.

"I feel a renewed energy and passion in many of the people we engage," Ali reports.

"The number of employee complaints has decreased by forty percent over the last year, and the results of the Engagement Survey suggest that eighty percent of employees feel engaged and valued," Priscilla chimes in.

"Wow, that is great news!" Jim responds.

The team confirms their virtual work plans and wraps up their meeting.

Jim heads back to his office to tie up a few loose ends. He fires off several emails and checks in with Rebecca before leaving. Over the next year, the agency will operate virtually with a few staff and key management personnel, including Jim, coming in two to three days a week.

On the way home, Jim and Prof-I discuss Jim's progress as a leader and his impact on his staff and the agency. Jim reiterates his appreciation for Prof-I and the support he has provided him.

"I'm thankful that you were willing to trust me to be a part of your journey, responds Prof-I. Our relationship and time together helped me immensely as well. It was meaningful for me as I felt valued; it reaffirmed my life's purpose to help others find their leadership voice. This is a great segue into what I wanted to discuss with you.

Jim sits silently as he waits for Prof-I to continue.

This ride concludes our journey together. Maybe our paths will cross in the future or another place. You have grown so much as a leader. Now you must continue practicing our lessons and live and lead the way you want others to remember you."

"Wow! that was a bit heavy. I feel like I'm losing a close friend. Will I be able to call you if I need advice?" he asks.

Prof-I smiles before responding.

"I promise I won't disappear. I'll be here if you need me."

Jim is a bit puzzled by his response but says nothing. They pull up to his house; he gets out of the cab simultaneously with Prof-I. The two men hug and exchange goodbyes.

Leadership Actions for Commissioning Others

- Work with others to identify their strengths and opportunities for development.

- Use delegation as a tool or approach for developing versus dumping.

- Demonstrate trust and confidence in employees, their expertise, and the areas you have empowered them to lead.

- Show support for the decisions employees make.

- Be clear about the 'what'—goals and expectations —but empower staff to determine the how—the approach for achieving the 'what.'

- Acknowledge employees' successes, and coach them on their challenges.

Chapter Seven: Consider Your Leadership Legacy

"Show up the way you want others to remember you!"

It's 7 a.m., and Jim is sitting in his office, reflecting on the past year and a half. Today is the first day that people can come back to the office. He smiles as he thinks about the challenges he and his team have faced and their effect on the agency. Jim does not downplay his failures, but he relishes the lessons he has learned from them. He chuckles, thinking about his first meeting with Rebecca when she asked him to take the position.

This was not a part of his career plans. He was content in his role as a director and retiring at that level. There were days over the past several months when he asked himself, *"What the hell was I thinking?"* Those days are in his rear-view mirror. He's come to realize that not all leaders volunteer for an assignment: sometimes, they are thrust into leadership based on the situation or what others see in them. He acknowledges that stepping into a management title is one thing but showing up as a leader is different and extraordinary. It's a transformative journey that must be consciously embraced. Once you have accepted the challenge, you must also accept that there will be trials and tribulations along with accomplishments and triumphs. These experiences sculpt leaders. There are two choices: wither in the heat of demands or forge a leadership identity and make your mark in the world by positively impacting those you serve and those who choose to follow you. Jim's reflection is interrupted by a knock on his door.

"Come in. You're here early," he says.

"I wanted to get a jump on things since this is the first day the office is fully open," replied Marie, his executive assistant.

"Yes, we still have a few things to clear up for staff. People are unsure how our hybrid approach is supposed to work."

"I thought leadership went over things during the virtual all-staff meeting."

"We did, but this is new for everyone, so we must be prepared to answer questions until people find their footing. That will take some time," states Jim.

They spend the next twenty minutes reviewing his schedule and agree to move things around to allow him to be available to support the other divisions during the first day of the transition back to the office.

After Marie leaves, Jim dives into his day, responding to emails and prepping for his 10:00 a.m. meeting with Rebecca. As he does so, he continues to reflect on his relationship with Prof-I and the difference it has made in his life, not just as a leader but as an individual. He realizes the two are intertwined and acknowledges that viewing himself as a whole person versus compartmentalizing his life has allowed him to be a healthy leader: mentally, emotionally, spiritually, and physically.

Being a healthy leader has allowed him to show up for others in ways that support their needs. He is grateful for the relationships with his co-workers and feels a debt of gratitude to Prof-I and is moved to tell him so. Jim picks up his phone to call Prof-I and is stunned to realize he doesn't have his phone number. *"All those months, he was just always there."*

By now, nothing surprised Jim about Prof-I. He calls the cab company where Prof-I works.

"Hello, EZ Ride Taxi; how can I help you?"

"Hi, I need to contact one of your drivers; I realize I don't have his cell number."

"They don't usually give customers their number. Do you have a complaint?"

"No, quite the opposite. He's been extremely helpful to me in a big way, and I would like to thank him."

"Oh, I see. We always appreciate customer feedback. I've been with the company since it started forty years ago, and very few customers ever call to say thank you for their experience. What's his name?"

"His name is Prof-I."

There is a moment's silence, and then...

"Is this a joke?" the person asks in annoyance.

"What do you mean? asks Jim, uncertain about the person's attitude. I really would like to thank him. He's helped me immensely over the past eighteen months."

"Sir, let me get this straight. You've been riding with Prof-I?"

"Yes, the Jamaican guy."

"Sir, I know whom you are referring to, and that simply isn't possible."

"Why is that?"

The man lets out a weary sigh.

"Prof-I has been dead for twenty years. We get these calls about every five years since he passed. He was one of the company's founders, but he wanted to keep driving even though he did not need to."

Jim is lost for words.

"Are you there?"

Jim responds, still in a daze.

"Yeah, I'm still here. Thank you and goodbye."

Jim sits back in his chair, stunned! He recalls his time spent with Prof-I. The conversations, Prof-I's carefree attitude, and, most distinctly, how people stared at the cab as they drove by. As Jim pieces things together, he's unsure of his feelings. He puts them aside to re-examine later and goes to his meeting with Rebecca.

Jim arrives at Rebecca's office a few minutes early, and she takes the opportunity to thank him for his leadership and work over the last eighteen months.

"I owe you a debt of gratitude. I can honestly say that watching you has forced me to look at how I lead and make some adjustments, and I hear the same from your colleagues on the executive team. They have all made changes in how they organize and lead their teams. Paul from finance has started a monthly listening session to hear from the employees in his division and has made quite a few changes based on ideas or concerns they've shared. Honestly, Jim, your leadership style and approach have been infectious. There's a buzz around this place. We may become an employer of choice after all. Have you seen the latest numbers on our employee-engagement survey?"

"Yes, I reviewed them last week with our team and at our all-staff division meeting. One of the consistent things we heard from staff working from home was that they appreciate the increased communication and engagement from the leadership team."

After discussing a few other issues on her agenda, Rebecca drops a bombshell.

"Jim, I want to talk to you about the primary reason for this meeting."

"What do you mean?"

"I have not shared this with anyone else on the team.

Jim sits up and braces himself.

I'm leaving the agency in six months, and I would like you to replace me as commissioner."

Jim is overwhelmed.

"Why me?"

"Why not you? You have inspired the agency with your leadership, and others are emulating you. Everyone is talking about you and your impact on how we view our work and the people we serve. Your forward thinking about working virtually allowed us to transition to working from home smoothly. Some of the other agencies had a tough time."

Jim sits quietly for a few seconds before responding.

"I need some time to think about this. It's a major step. I need to talk it over with my family, and more importantly, I need to pray on this one."

This time, Rebecca is respectful of Jim's needs.

"You have some time with this one. As I said, I will be leaving six months from now. I would like to affirm your nomination with the mayor in about thirty days.

Jim extends his hand; Rebecca hugs him instead.

You are not only a good leader, Jim, but also a good person."

On his way back to his office, Jim ponders Rebecca's request. Thinking about her offer causes him to recall his experience with Prof-I and his discovery that he has been dead for twenty years. Both circumstances feel overwhelming, but despite learning about Prof-I, he wishes he could talk to him about this latest development. Arriving at his office, he finds a stack of messages from Marie and spends the following few hours returning phone calls and responding to emails.

Marie interrupts him.

"Jim, have you forgotten the leadership meeting with your team? They are waiting in the conference room."

"I am on my way," he responds as he gathers his notepad and agenda. Jim greets his leadership team with a big smile. This is the first time they've all physically shared the same space since the pandemic started. Ali shows off his new beard and endures the friendly teasing of his peers. After sharing some of the things they did while working from home, the team gets down to business.

"We need to discuss the various work options available to staff and figure out how we will support them. Fifty-three percent of our employees have opted to work full-time in the building. Thirty percent chose the hybrid model of two to three days a week in the office, and everyone else will remain in full work-from-home status," Jim informs the team.

"Why didn't we just have everyone return to work so we could run things as we did before the pandemic? asks Juan. My team has revised the space plan several times since the three work options were announced."

"There is no going back to the way things were, Jim replies. If agencies choose to do so, they did not learn anything from the crisis we just faced. Let's push forward by leveraging the lessons we learned during the pandemic."

They each share their arrangements for supporting the agency's post-pandemic work plan. Priscilla is a bit concerned about the employees who are required to have more presence in the office but may not wish to do so.

"I'm working with Legal and Labor to hash out the particulars. We are anticipating some legal and labor-related actions from some employees, but we will be fine. We plan to follow CDC and state guidelines."

Feeling good about his team's information, Jim thanks everyone for their work and commitment. They stick around a few more minutes, bantering and checking on each other's wellness.

"Well, guys, I've got to run; I need to take care of a few things before I leave today," Jim informs them.

Instead of the usual remarks, they share high fives and hugs. It is as if they missed the camaraderie they fostered before the lockdown.

Priscilla shares heartfelt sentiments of gratitude to Jim for his leadership and trust and thanks him for empowering her and allowing her to find her voice. She is a bit choked up, but with a smile, she adds,

"You guys know I'm not a mushy person, but I have never felt as energized and engaged as I have over the last eighteen months."

"No speech from me, Jim says, but I want to thank you for trusting me. We all did this together. I am a better leader because you all agreed to follow and lead in your own ways."

Eventually, they return to their respective offices to finish up the day.

In his office, Jim is tying up some loose ends while reflecting on today's meetings and taking stock of his leadership's impact on his team and the agency. He thinks about Prof-I but cannot reconcile what the man at the cab company shared with him. "Am I dreaming all of this? How is it possible for me to not only have conversations with someone who has been dead for twenty years but also to ride to and from work with him for eighteen months?" Dazed, Jim looks at the clock and packs up his things. He requests an Uber, as he did this morning. The app lets him know that the driver was 10 minutes away.

Downstairs, the driver is waiting. Jim gets in the car.

"Hey, she says, remembering him from this morning. Thanks for the five-star rating earlier, your tip paid for my lunch."

"I appreciated the customer service," Jim smiles.

He retrieves a report from his bag and begins to review it for an important meeting tomorrow. Immersed in the information, he highlights a few points. Feeling the car swerve, Jim looks up.

"Are you okay?"

Looking a bit tired, she responds,

"I'm okay; I had to avoid a pothole."

Jim returns to his reading.

A few minutes later, the car swerves again. Jim looks up, but this time he braces himself as he sees the car heading straight for a pickup truck. The two vehicles collide, and Jim is knocked unconscious.

Within 10 minutes, Jim is extricated and taken to the emergency room. The room is crowded with medical personnel. The hospital uses his identification to locate and contact his wife. Within the hour, Pam and the children are at the hospital.

"When can we see Daddy?" asks Ben.

Marcia is quiet and holds her mother's hand tightly.

Jim stirs.

"Why am I here?"

"You've been in an accident, and we are going to make sure you are okay," one of the doctors tells him.

They leave and then the door opens again.

"It's you! How?" Jim asks incredulously.

"I know you have many questions; Prof-I responds. Let's take a walk."

"I can't; I was injured in an accident."

"You'll be fine, trust me."

Jim gets up and walks with Prof-I to the end of the hallway, where they get in the elevator.

"Where are we going?"

"We're going up."

Jim notices only two buttons, 'Up' and 'Down.' He's confused but says nothing. As they begin their ride up, Prof-I begins to speak.

"I know you contacted the cab company, and they shared with you that I passed many years ago. It's true."

Jim becomes a little anxious and more confused.

"Then how is it possible that you are here? How is it possible that you drove me back and forth to work and home for the past eighteen months?"

Prof-I explains how Jim and others before him could see and talk with him.

"You needed guidance in your leadership journey. You accepted the call when Rebecca asked you to step up and lead. You were a little reluctant at first, but you accepted the challenge. You are one of those people who possess the necessary qualities, like open-mindedness, service orientation, and humility. Most importantly, you're willing to accept that there are attributes you don't possess but are open to learning. You are also steadfast in your values. This made it easy to unlock the leader within you. You see, Jim, essentially, there are two types of people. The first are those who run to leadership for the title, fame, money, and all the surface trappings. In their minds, leadership is all about satisfying their personal needs and ego. Then there are people like you who are committed to making a difference and elevating others. You are not attracted to the surface trappings of what some refer to as leadership. You may lack the confidence, and yet you go about the business of making a difference and serving something greater than yourself. I responded to your inner call for help and answers to the burning question about how to lead others."

"When are we going back down?"

"We're not. Your work here is done. You've made your mark on the people you care about, your agency, and the people it serves."

"What do you mean, we're not going back down?" Jim asks with trepidation.

"Jim, you didn't make it. You died in the accident."

"But the doctor said I was fine."

"That's not what she meant. She said that you are fine now. Your work is complete."

Jim drops to his knees and begins to cry.

"I have so much more to do."

Prof-I puts his hand on Jim's shoulder and gently says,

"There's always more to do while we are on earth. Everyone has a beginning and an end. We just prefer not to think or talk about it. People live as if they will be here forever. That's not the case. We must make every day count, taking full advantage of the small things while we enjoy the big things that come our way."

"What about Pam, the kids?" asks Jim mournfully.

"They'll be fine; you made sure of that. You laid a great foundation by being a role model to your children. You have ensured they can live comfortably with your savings, pension, personal investments, and more. Pam will manage. She'll find a way to make things happen."

"He's coding!" the nurse in the operating room announces.

The medical team works feverishly on Jim, to no avail, and they pronounce him dead.

"Time of death, 9:30 pm."

"I'll go out and talk to his family," one of the doctors says.

As the doctor approaches, Pam, who can tell something is wrong by the look on the doctor's face, screams in anguish.

"Nooo!"

When the doctor hugs her, the children sense that something is wrong and begin to cry. Eventually, Pam is calm enough to take the children home.

The next day the news of Jim's death circulates the agency. People are shocked, hurt, and devastated. His team spends the day in his conference room in a daze, crying and supporting each other. Rebecca joins them after spending time with members of the executive team.

"I am here if any of you would like to talk; also, Priscilla, would you reach out to a grief counselor to support staff who may need it?"

Over the next few days, Jim's family arranges his memorial service. They reach out to Rebecca and Jim's team, informing them of the date and time and asking if his friends and colleagues would say a few words. Ali volunteers to take the lead in identifying people and helping Pam with putting the program together. They agree upon a theme:

"JIM REYNOLDS—The Legacy of a Great Person Who Became a Great Leader."

It's the day of the memorial service. Due to social distancing requirements, the auditorium is filled with friends, family, and others who have logged in virtually. Jim's picture is projected onto two large screens; Pam decided not to have a viewing, knowing that he would not want to be remembered that way.

"She remembered," says Jim, standing in the back of the room with Prof-I.

"What do you mean?"

"I once told her that if anything ever happened to me, I did not want to be on display like some object or like the shell of the person who was once full of life."

The program begins with a prayer and opening remarks. At the reading of Jim's eulogy, some people nod their heads and reflect on the man and what he meant to them. When the speaker finishes, the attendees are invited to share their memories of Jim. One by one, people take to the podium and talk about their relationship with Jim. His integrity, willingness to put others first, and his commitment to engage those that others considered 'the little people,' are honored.

Rebecca manages to share their last conversation and her request for Jim to take her place as commissioner before being overcome with emotion. Jim's team stepped up to the podium together and shared how he helped them find their individual and collective leadership voice and how their division is in a much better place.

"I feel good about the last time I met with them. We hugged, and I let them know how much I appreciated them as individuals and the work they do for the agency and the communities we serve. It felt like the right thing to do." Says Jim.

"That's great! One of the principles I used to live by is if you ever get the urge to do something good, do it. Letting them know how you felt at that moment was the right thing to do," Prof-I responds.

As the last speaker wrapped his tribute, a young woman walked up to the podium and introduced herself.

"Hello, I'm Kenya, and I would like to tell you about the impact Jim had on my life. Up until two years ago, I worked in the mailroom and struggled to pay for school. One day, while dropping off a package at the mailroom, Jim noticed my books and asked what I was studying. I told him public administration and about how I hoped to move up in the agency one day. He made me feel comfortable enough to share that I was a single parent struggling to pay for school. Later that day, Jim sent me a link to an organization that helps single mothers pay for their education. I finished school and got a job as an executive assistant with the finance division director. Jim always inquired how things were going when he saw me, and I later learned that he had put in a good word for me with the finance director, but he never mentioned it.

Until recently, many of us felt invisible to upper management. That changed because of Jim Reynolds. We now feel like we are business partners in the agency. We feel like we are an essential part of the mission," Kenya concludes.

Kenya's tribute touches Jim.

"It appears you had more of an impact on people than you thought. That was more than just your everyday leadership. You brought a human perspective to the idea of leading others, which has created a community of leaders at all levels of the agency," suggests Prof-I.

"Well, I remember someone telling me that leadership had nothing to do with my title; it was about influencing and inspiring people who wanted to be a part of something special," responds Jim.

"And that, my friend, was the key to building your leadership legacy. As you can tell from the testimonials, they will never forget you and how you led them."

After the service ends, people stay for a while, indulging in small talk and spending time with Jim's family. As the crowd dwindles, Pam speaks to Jim's team.

"Thank you all for your help and support," she says tearfully.

"We are all part of Jim's family, which makes us a part of your family," Stacy reassures her.

They exchange comforting hugs. As the family leaves the building, Ben, Jim's son, turns around, looks back, and sees his dad standing next to Prof-I. He pauses before waving. Jim smiles, waves back, turns, and walks into a soft, glowing light with Prof-I. He realizes his work is done and feels at peace.

Considering Your Leadership Legacy

- Describe the type of leader you want to become. How do you want others to remember you as a leader?

- What leadership qualities and behaviors do you currently demonstrate that support your leadership legacy?

- What leadership qualities and behaviors do you currently demonstrate that may hurt your leadership legacy?

- What do you need to do, starting today, to build or strengthen your leadership legacy?

ACKNOWLEDGEMENTS

To Prof-I Reynolds of Ocho Rios, Jamaica, a natural philosopher, thank you for listening and providing a balm for the soul.

Troy Lambert, I appreciate you taking the time to collaborate with me on designing a cover that conveys what I want to communicate.

To my coach, Jennifer McMenamin, the kick in the pants came just when I needed it.

Dr. Joseph E. Bavaria, thank you for saving my life not once but twice. God has blessed you with the gift of being the best cardiothoracic surgeon in the world.

To my sister and editor, Rowena Rolton-McGann, you have always been a role model for me. I am proud to receive your stamp of approval.

To all my family and friends, thank you for your decades of love and support.